Walking

with

the

Shepherd

Walking

with ~

~ *the*

Shepherd

ISABEL ANDERS

OLIVER
NELSON

THOMAS NELSON PUBLISHERS
NASHVILLE

Published in Nashville, Tennessee, by Thomas Nelson, Inc.,
Publishers, and distributed in Canada by Word
Communications, Ltd., Richmond, British Columbia.

The Bible version used in this publication is THE NEW KING
JAMES VERSION. Copyright © 1979, 1980, 1982,
Thomas Nelson, Inc., Publishers.

Library of Congress Cataloging-in-Publication Data

Anders, Isabel, 1946–
    Walking with the shepherd / Isabel Anders.
        p.   cm.
    Includes bibliographical references.
    ISBN 0-8407-9402-9
    1. Bible.   O.T.   Psalms XXIII—Meditations.   I. Title.
BS145023rd   1994
223'.206—dc20   93-47218
                                                      CIP

Printed in the United States of America.

        1 2 3 4 5 6 — 99 98 97 96 95 94

For Bill,
whose love is to me green pastures and still waters.

I also thank my father,
whose lifelong love and reading of the Psalms has
so enriched my life; and I would like to express my
appreciation to Mary Ruth Woodard for her
friendship and special encouragement on
this project.

Contents

Introduction   *xiii*

1. The Life That Lacks Nothing   *1*

2. The Place of True Peace   *17*

3. Restored and Refreshed   *31*

4. Troubled but Not Forsaken   *45*

5. A Well-Attended Feast   *59*

6. All That We Truly Need   *71*

7. Grace for the Journey   *83*

8. Coming Home   *95*

Bibliography   *105*

Psalm 23

The Lord the Shepherd of His People

A PSALM OF DAVID.

The Lord is my shepherd;
   I shall not want.
He makes me to lie down in green pastures;
He leads me beside the still waters.
He restores my soul;
He leads me in the paths of righteousness
   For His name's sake.

Yea, though I walk through the valley
   of the shadow of death,
I will fear no evil;
For You are with me;
Your rod and Your staff,
   they comfort me.

You prepare a table before me in the
   presence of my enemies;
You anoint my head with oil;
My cup runs over.
Surely goodness and mercy shall
   follow me
All the days of my life;
And I will dwell in the house
   of the LORD
Forever.

PSALM 23 is the world's favourite psalm. It is the favourite of Jew, Eastern Orthodox, Western Protestant, and wistful agnostic alike. It comes alive when used at a wedding, even more so when said or sung at a funeral. And it expresses more vividly than any other portion of Scripture the individual's private experience of God's grace.

> —George A. F. Knight, *Psalms*, Vol. 1,
> The Daily Study Bible Series

KNOWLEDGE is the process of piling up facts. Wisdom lies in their simplification.

> —Martin H. Fischer

THE sweet word "shepherd" . . . brings when [we] read it or hear it, as it were a confidence, a consolation, or security like the word "father."

> —Martin Luther

Introduction

*T*he Shepherd Psalm. The very words conjure up for most of us a somewhat idyllic setting: a peaceful meadow in the peak of spring. The sun is shining. It is a *pastoral* scene in the literal meaning of the word: relating to sheep and shepherds—but so often understood also as relating to spiritual care or guidance.

This much-loved psalm of sheep and the Shepherd is a wonderful storehouse of comfort and understanding for anyone seeking inner peace and the wisdom of God's guidance. It begins at a very necessary starting point: our acknowledgment that we need Someone to walk with us and be our Source of strength. "The Lord is my shepherd," and from there a new experience of opening up to love begins.

We are not alone! The ancient writer (this psalm is traditionally attributed to King David of Israel) is not so far removed from us and our concerns today. We pray, as did the psalm-ist, to be led—daily, carefully, through life's path—and to the safety of God's dwelling place.

In the beautiful, vivid lines of poetry which make up this psalm, we can learn something of the nature of God, our Lord and Shepherd; and we will also discover the flavor and tenor of our relationship to Him and to each other as sheep of His flock.

We will see what it is that God provides and what we receive by being in relationship to our Shepherd—intimately, in commitment and thoroughly grounded peace.

Let's imagine the scene a little more fully and think about how it might apply to our longing for such companionship. Perhaps the spring lambs have just been born. There are always some who are newborn in their aware-ness of their need of God—it might well be ourselves. At any rate, we rejoice whenever new people have been awakened to come and join with us on our journey.

In this picture there is a certain contentment and delight, an innocent peace in the air. There

are also playfulness, enjoyment of the green-
ness, sweetness of the earth, and the freedom
of belonging to the flock of a caring shepherd.

As we think of the shepherd's world, we are
reminded of an earlier, perhaps simpler, day
when more people earned their living on the
slopes of rolling hills—following a flock, tend-
ing to its needs as they occurred, with focused
attention and a loving heart.

We yearn to recover some of that sense of
peace and contentment in our daily, harried,
complicated lives!

In examining this psalm, we hope to discover what it can teach us of the nature of
walking daily in God's care and what is in store
for us in the future along this path. We will
look carefully at this song of David, line by
line, phrase by phrase. Each segment brings to
mind some aspect of our soul's relationship to
God, to the world, and to others we will inevi-
tably meet along the path.

As we take each step, let us ask God for the
few moments' peace, the time and the place,
and the heart attitude that will enable us to
stop in the middle of our busyness and stress,

our worries and problems. Then we can experience simply being God's children, God's sheep—trusting only God to lead and restore us to the joy of this one-on-One relationship which is possible in this moment, by faith.

But He made His own people go forth like sheep, and guided them in the wilderness like a flock; and He led them on safely, so that they did not fear (Ps. 78:52–53).

Walking
with
the
Shepherd

CHAPTER 1

THE LIFE THAT LACKS NOTHING

The LORD is my shepherd;
I shall not want.

ALL I NEED TO KNOW IS
THAT MY SHEPHERD IS
PRESENT TO ME NOW.

*P*EACE and comfort can be found nowhere except in simple obedience.

—Francois Fénelon

We all long to be safe, free of fear, living in an environment as close to our idea of paradise as possible. We yearn to discover the serenity and peace which is possible for *us*.

This is not escape! This is a normal, healthy desire—to claim happiness and live in fulfillment and safety. But how we go about attaining such a goal makes all the difference.

H. King Oehmig relates (in *Synthesis*, April 21, 1991) a provocative illustration from modern life of how one young couple with two attractive children were "upset with the life they had chosen. They were tired of the impact television was having on their children. They were fed up with undocumented sugar in cereals and the increasing amount of junk food being hoisted on an unsuspecting (sheepish?) culture. They had had it with the low integrity of the school system on top of excessive taxation."

In short, they were looking to return to some truly idyllic, pastoral spot on earth where they might personally reclaim an earlier vision and practice simplicity of life. The rat race they found themselves in,

though providing a good income, poisoned
the fabric of their family life. They
had read all the articles about Type A's and
heart disease, along with the horrors
of tapwater causing cancer. They knew the
divorce rate was spiraling out of control.
... So the couple went to the library and
began to take life into their own hands.

For a year they researched the world,
examining the places best suited for
raising a family away from society's
pollutants... where they could develop
to their full potential in a healthful,
environmentally sound, stress-free place.

When they left their home in New England for a small, isolated chain of islands off the coast of Argentina, they were filled with anticipation of just the life they longed for. Then the war in the Falkland Islands—their new home—broke out. And the rest is history.

The lesson here seems to be that—however deep may be our longing for another "place" to be and another chance at happiness: our best opportunity for wholeness and healing is probably right where we are. This is true because *wherever we are,* God is right here with us.

The psalm reminds us, in one of the most often quoted lines from Scripture: "The Lord is my shepherd." I recently saw a cartoon in which Dennis the Menace repeats to his parents what he thought he heard in church: "The Lord is my chauffeur, I shall not walk"!

"The Lord is my shepherd; I shall not want." The phrasing was confusing to me when I was a child. What was it that I wasn't supposed to *want*? Surely not the guidance and presence of the Shepherd—I wanted that presence very much! Gradually I became more accustomed to the poetry of the Psalms and the shades of truth which reach deep into our hearts as we let such phrases enter our understanding.

And as adults, it is when we begin to understand what we are being told here—*All I need to know is that my Shepherd is present to me now; I have everything I need*—that life begins to make sense. It is as though someone has suddenly added color to a black and white movie.

This truth is at once wonderfully simple and all-demanding in its implications. To come to the place in which we "want for nothing," or need nothing else, we first need to acknowledge the Source of all spiritual wealth and guidance, the One who walks beside us, dwells within us, and loves us as a shepherd does sheep.

Truly, for us as well as for the ancient writer of the psalm, God is our Guide. Knowing this is the starting point for acknowledging the kingdom of God, which surrounds and includes us.

"The Lord is my shepherd." To enter into the truth of any poetry, we must enter into the figure of speech. We need to accept, as much as is possible, the world to which it allows us entry. Here it is a world of pastoral concern, careful guidance, and continuing care by a loving Shepherd who takes into account our well-being at every step.

Columnist Barbara Reynolds has written in her syndicated column (*The Tennessean,* Aug. 11, 1991) of a time when she desperately needed guidance. She had somewhat pridefully resigned from a secure job to go and start her own news service.

"I was my own boss and it felt good" for a while, she writes. "But it wasn't long before I felt like the greatest loser who'd ever lived." Suddenly, a nationwide economic downturn wiped out all her contracts with the newspapers for which she regularly wrote.

"A worried brow replaced a triumphant smile.... I often dreamed I was a bag lady. Many of my so-called friends forsook me; several who remained were jobless themselves. We often joked we were too poor to buy a crippled fly a toothpick crutch. I was so down I believed stray dogs no longer thought I was important enough to bark at."

But Ms. Reynolds' response to her misfortune was to take time to look within herself, to learn compassion, and to seek God's guidance.

"I asked God what I should do with the rest of my life and to lead me there. I also promised never to forget the bridge that brought me across." That bridge was her faith in God's goodness. She quotes one Bible verse which especially helped her, Isaiah 40:31: "Those who wait on the LORD shall renew their strength; they shall mount up with wings like eagles, they shall run and not be weary, they shall walk and not faint."

How wonderful to find such a testimony to God's grace in the pages of the morning newspaper! Reynolds eventually found a better job than she had ever had before, and she remembered to give thanks for the guidance which had led her through the valley of loss to that very position.

Many of us also have stories of loss and restoration that end happily (though not without the remembrance of depletion and mourning). Some have not yet found exactly the place they wish to be, where their gifts can be most effectively used. *But God the Shepherd is still leading, still walking with each of us.*

If we are able to affirm that we are not alone, as Ms. Reynolds and her other unemployed friends were able to do—with good humor, in the faithfulness of companionship—then there is hope for us as well. The pastures we may find ourselves in right now are perhaps not exactly to our liking. Maybe we feel crowded in on all sides by the needs of others—so that no one recognizes our individual worth. Perhaps we feel unappreciated, unnoticed, unloved. Sheep are not often singled out for their individuality or specialness.

This timeless psalm is a wonderful reminder that we are specially loved by our Maker and our Master. Jesus said, "When he brings out his own sheep, he goes before them; and the sheep follow him, for they know his voice" (John 10:4). And, "He calls his own sheep by name and leads them out" (v. 3).

Out of trouble, safe from the fangs of the wolf, through an open gate to the sheepfold, into the life for which they were intended— this guidance is what Jesus promises us.

As with any metaphor or word picture, the sheep and shepherd image does not hold up or apply to our complex lives at every point. But it does offer a poignancy which touches our imaginations and answers our deepest needs. Such care provides a context for survival and nurturing which is available in green pastures—where food is abundant and both safety and community are available to us.

We are, of course, challenged to go far beyond the example of sheep in our growth toward greater self-esteem and in the Christian life, using our personal gifts in our own situation. We want to be nourished and strengthened in these positive ways while we learn to minimize bad habits and grow into sounder thinking and healthier attitudes.

The apostle Paul referred to such natural growth as being able to digest the "meat" of the Word of God, weaning ourselves from the pure milk which gave us our start in this new life (see 1 Cor. 3:2; Heb. 5:12–14). But we all must begin somewhere!

Perhaps we need, from time to time, simply to contemplate the simplicity of the pure milk, the pure guidance, the simple walk with our Lord. We need to return to a savoring of the one-on-One experience which a personal relationship with God implies. In this relationship, it is as though all of our needs are already anticipated by our Shepherd, all our wants are considered, and we need not strive for an elusive "more" all of the time.

"The Lord is my shepherd." The comparison of God to a shepherd occurs also in the book of Isaiah the prophet: "He will feed His flock like a shepherd; He will gather the lambs with His arm, and carry them in His bosom, and gently lead those who are with young" (40:11). What a beautiful picture of compassion and nurturing we are given here—of the God who just a few verses earlier in the chapter is also called one with a "strong arm," who will rule with a "strong hand."

This is the multifaceted portrait of the Shepherd, Almighty God, that Scripture presents to us. God, our Guide, is both strong enough to protect and defend (as we will also see later in the psalm) and gentle enough to bring forth safely those who are still weak and dependent—perhaps some who still harbor doubts about the life with God.

God is our Shepherd—everything we need. And this God is present to us now in our just beginning, or steadily continuing, or many years' experience of healing. God is there to relieve us from whatever difficulties or trying circumstances we have been able to acknowledge and seek help to overcome.

Psychiatrist Gerald G. May, in his book *The Awakened Heart*, suggests the concept of "stretching and yielding" as a wonderful spiritual response to God and as the alternative to our own willfulness. Perhaps we have already seen that whatever *we* willed for ourselves has brought us more fear and less control. And so, we find we must stretch—and yield:

"We can stretch our minds without feeling we must comprehend everything. We are stretched by the circumstances in which we find ourselves, and we can choose to stretch ourselves in meeting them. We can stretch our wills forward in intention, stretch open our hearts in consecration."

But, he warns, stretching alone is pointless and must always be followed by *yielding*. This means yielding to the superior knowledge, love, and care of God, who sees the larger picture and our place and purpose within it. Thinking we know what is best for ourselves, without consulting our Lord and Guide, can consistently get us into trouble.

May counsels us to notice "how infants stretch and yield, how relaxed they are when asleep, how vital when awake. The reason is, *they are not working against themselves* [italics mine]. Natural stretching and yielding flow in harmony." And both are part of our dependence and trust in the Shepherd who walks beside us.

We too must learn not to work against ourselves! This means being willing to be stretched by our circumstances, by new challenges, by considering others around us.

And it also will demand yielding, as Barbara Reynolds did, to the pain or loneliness or heartache which may be a legitimate response to the reality we are faced with. She found she had to fully *taste* and *experience* the despair of joblessness, for the duration of that trial.

But what joy and fulfillment lies ahead for us—as it did for that courageous and insightful woman—when we learn to trust our Shepherd!

Ask Yourself:

Am I conscious of God's presence with me and for me, working for my good and the good of others around me, right now? "And we know that all things work together for good to those who love God, to those who are the called according to His purpose" (Rom. 8:28).

Can I point to ways in which I have been led into greater, fuller life?

Can I trust my Shepherd now, in my present circumstances, to be still with me, the Source of my strength and comfort, through this day, this week, this specific testing?

CHAPTER *2*

THE PLACE OF TRUE PEACE

He makes me to lie down in green pastures; He leads me beside the still waters.

RESTING IN MY PRESENT CIRCUMSTANCES, BECOMING COMFORTABLE WITH MY OWN COMPANY, IS A NECESSARY PART OF MY GROWTH.

*T*HE Shepherd knows what pastures are best for His sheep, and they must not question nor doubt, but trustingly follow Him. Perhaps He sees that the best pastures for some are to be found in the midst of opposition or of earthly trials. If He leads you there, you may be sure they are green for you, and you will grow and be made strong by feeding there. Perhaps He sees that the best waters for you to walk beside will be raging waves of trouble and sorrow. If this should be the case, He will make them still waters for you, and you must go and lie down beside them, and let them have all their blessed influences upon you.

—H. W. Smith

*I*T is the very pursuit of happiness that thwarts happiness.

—Viktor E. Frankl

*O*NE of life's gifts is that each of us, no matter how tired and downtrodden, finds reasons for thankfulness.

—J. Robert Maskin

*B*ritish author and missionary Hannah Hurnard, author of the classic allegory *Hinds' Feet on High Places*, wrote beautifully of her conversion experience as a young woman—when the God she had heard about all her life finally became real to her:

He is real. He is here. He loves me.... I am perfectly safe.... I was still the old Hannah, but in some miraculous and mysterious way I had been lifted into a completely new mental and spiritual environment, out of the border land of outer darkness, into the light and glory of heaven. It was as though a miserable, stunted plant had suddenly been transplanted from a tiny flowerpot, into a sunny, richly fertilized flowerbed. I was lifted out of the dreadful isolation of self-imprisonment and set down in the love of God.

"Or," she continues in another comparison, "it was like being lifted out of a winter land of ice and desolation, to be set down in a summer land of light and flowers and bird-song" (*Hearing Heart*, Tyndale House, 1978, pp. 26–27).

"He makes me to lie down in green pastures." This is the experience of so many people who can also say with the psalmist, "You have set my feet in a wide place" (31:8).

An unknown author wrote the following lines of this assurance of God's care:

> Never a day goes by
> But something new I know—
> The blessing of strength restored
> For the way God would have me go.

When we acknowledge the presence of God in our lives, as Shepherd and Guide, we see everything around us in a different light. The astonishing thing about this awakening, which is occurring among people at many stages of life and in many different ways, is that *God is here and not elsewhere.*

This restoration to a healthier way of looking at ourselves, our circumstances, those around us, and the possibilities in our own given situation can come in an *instant*.

It is like waking up in a field that had looked to us desolate, without promise of life or even survival for another day. We may blink at the sun, which seems perhaps brighter and more illuminating. Gradually, the landscape around us comes into clearer focus. It may be familiar—and even comfortingly ordinary to us—when we see it. Yet in our heart we find that we are experiencing *blessing within our very circumstances* because it is in that place, at that moment, that we have turned to God for help.

An inner peace becomes possible, a focus on the slice of reality in which we dwell at that instant in time. Yet, writes Esther deWaal in *Seeking God*, "for most of us the place does matter and to begin with it is much easier to find God in the countryside than in an overcrowded supermarket." She says, "We in the world"—compared to the monk who lives in a monastery—"live lives punctuated by the constant expectations of a busy life which, from the ringing of the alarm in the morning until the turning of the latch in the door at night, is made up of situations, encounters, demands which we often would never have chosen and would much prefer to evade if we could. *Yet it is just within these limitations that we shall find God*" (italics mine).

How are we to awaken to green pastures, to still waters, within our very own circumstances? We seek stability, acceptance, and a gentle yielding to our Shepherd that can transform our perception—and indeed, our very lives—in this way.

We are sometimes told by our pastor or spiritual leader to rest in the moment, to stop in our eager desire to push forward and find immediate answers. My pastor would sometimes play soft, worshipful music without words for the first five minutes of a gathering. Added to this was a time of quiet heart preparation; a reading of a short passage of Scripture together; and specific prayer for an *open heart* and a *clear mind* to receive what God would reveal to us in such a time of seeking guidance.

Sometimes the gift we receive is—as the psalmist so marvelously expressed—beyond our asking or even our imagining. We may fear turning to God, initially, because of what might be required of us that we don't wish to give up.

C. S. Lewis wrote in his memoir of his wife Helen Joy Davidman, *A Grief Observed*:

> All sorts of mistakes are possible when you are dealing with [God]. Long ago, before we were married, H. was haunted all one morning as she went about her work with the obscure sense of God (so to speak) "at her elbow," demanding her attention. And of course, not being a perfected saint, she had the feeling that it would be a question, as it usually is, of some unrepented sin or tedious duty. At last she gave in—I know how one puts it off—and faced Him. But the message was "I want to *give* you something," and instantly she entered into joy.

Resting in our present circumstances does not mean refusing to budge, being reluctant to change, stubbornly staying put, regardless of the circumstances. In fact, the rest or refreshment or new perspective that we are given as a gift—as Helen was given instantaneous joy—may be a preparation for what is to come next in our lives. It may be a further grounding in our experience of being led by our Shepherd that will help to make us more secure, wiser, surer of who it is that we follow and seek. Then, when the next round of difficulties arises, we may be able to see those difficulties as challenges in our new life rather than mere pitfalls.

Times of enjoyment and assurance, of stretching ourselves and yielding to God, are as essential to our spiritual journey as are the rigors of our daily work, our humdrum tasks, our planning for the future. Psalm 16, a psalm of David, speaks of the difference it makes to dwell with "the LORD always before me": "Because He is at my right hand I shall not be moved. Therefore my heart is glad, and my glory rejoices; My flesh also will rest in hope" (vv. 8–9).

Rest and peace within our bodies constitute

an important part of our total well-being, which we experience physically as well as spiritually—sometimes in dramatic ways. We are literally to rest in God, as though supported by invisible wires of connection, or by the "everlasting arms," as Scripture puts it (Deut. 33:27).

Some of us like to imagine ourselves surrounded by God's care in the form of guardian angels, and indeed, there is biblical support for this understanding (see Ps. 91:11; Num. 22:22–27).

If God is here for us and not elsewhere, then in fact *this place* is holy and *this moment* is sacred. We are encompassed by God's care in the form of the many things that sustain our physical life: air to breathe, food to eat, shelter, warmth, companionship, work to do...love, if we are so blessed.

Yet part of our task is to become comfortable with this sense of staying put to see what God will do with such unpromising material as we sometimes feel we are. We wonder how God can make gold out of the roomful of straw in which we are sure that we live, or transform the very atmosphere around us that seems to be killing our spirit and making it impossible for us to go on.

One friend of mine, who was going through the almost unbearable strains of a broken relationship, would take her Bible to bed with her at night and put it under her pillow, grasping it in the night for tangible assurance that God's promises *for her* were still solid and dependable. And by God's grace, she survived to become a wonderful witness to God's love and care. She couldn't see the green pastures then, but they revealed themselves to her in time.

She went *slowly* through that time of trial and decision making, and her patience affected the course of her family and their lives from then on. She took time (as she later urged me to go slowly in my own difficult situation), and gradually she became able to bear the losses, to face the prospect of continuing without a loved one. The turbulent waters of her life became again the still waters of comfort and sustaining peace.

Where is the place of true peace? Esther deWaal quotes Catherine de Hueck Doherty in describing what it means to stand still in God's presence:

It is not a place, a geographical spot. It is not first and foremost a house or a room. It is within your heart. A woman pregnant goes about her daily business with the only difference between her and other people being that she is carrying a child. She carries that secret life round within her, and the mystery of this, which applies to both men and women, is that it is totally there whatever the external circumstances.

To know the presence of God, our Shepherd, as surely as we know our own presence! This awareness is necessary at this stage of growth so that we will have eyes to see and ears to hear the next words of instruction, or comfort, or guidance for the future.

When we can learn to hear our own heart-whispers and God's words of love to us in response—through Scripture, in prayer, and in the love others show us—we will indeed be in that place of green pastures and still waters.

Ask Yourself:

When I pray, do I spend all of my time telling God what to do; or have I learned also to be quiet, to rest in the moment I am in, and to listen for the "still small voice" (see 1 Kings 19:12)?

"As for me, I will see Your face.... I shall be satisfied when I awake..." (Ps. 17:15).

What are the green pastures and still waters that are nurturing and supporting my life right now? Have I given thanks for these gifts of God? Am I learning to recognize small tokens of grace even in the midst of troubles in my life?

"Love is a fruit in season at all times and within the reach of every hand. Anyone may gather it and no limit is set" (Mother Teresa of Calcutta).

Am I learning, increasingly, to give love as well as receive love?

CHAPTER 3

RESTORED AND REFRESHED

He restores my soul; He leads me in the paths of righteousness for His name's sake.

MY GROWING SENSE OF WHOLENESS IN GOD'S PRESENCE IS GROUNDED IN SELF-DISCOVERY, BASED ALWAYS ON TRUTH.

*W*HAT you are is God's gift to you; what you make of it is your gift to God.

—Anthony Dalla Villa

Author Frederick Buechner, in *The Magnificent Defeat*, retells a parable called "The Tiger":

Once there was a motherless tiger cub who was adopted by goats and brought up by them to speak their language, emulate their ways, eat their food, and in general to believe that he was a goat himself. Then one day a king tiger came along, and when the goats scattered in fear the young tiger was left alone to confront him, afraid and yet somehow not afraid.

The king tiger asked him what he meant by his unseemly masquerade, but all that the young one could do in response was to bleat nervously and continue nibbling at the grass. So the tiger carried him to a pool where he forced him to look at their two reflections side by side and draw his own conclusions.

When this failed, he offered him his first piece of raw meat. At first the young tiger recoiled from the unfamiliar taste of it, but then as he ate more and he began to feel it warming his blood, the truth gradually became clear to him.

Lashing his tail and digging his claws into the ground, the young beast finally raised his head high, and the jungle trembled at the sound of his exultant roar.

In a similar fashion, our journey with God is a path of discovery. Both the concepts—restoration and discovery—imply a return to an awareness or acceptance of something that must have been, in some sense, lost or forgotten.

Every one of us begins life as a unique expression of God, explain Kathleen V. Hurley and Theodore E. Dobson in their book *What's My Type?* "At the core of every person is a Divine Image, a strength signifying that each person is created whole and free. This whole and free person is born into a selfish world in which destructive attitudes control us from childhood on, leading us down the blind alleys of life."

The Bible describes the origin of this divine image in the words of God: "Let Us make man in Our image, according to Our likeness.... So God created man in His own image; in the image of God He created him; male and female He created them. Then God blessed them" (Gen. 1:26–28). It is the imprint of God's own nature and creativity that we bear.

When the psalmist writes, "He restores my soul," we feel the depth of this promise, which is being fulfilled in us *as we are* and *as we have learned to face ourselves*. Derek Kidner writes, "The retrieving or reviving of the sheep pictures the deeper renewal of the [person] of God, spiritually perverse or ailing as he may be." And J. Thornton adds, "The same hand which first rescued us from ruin, reclaims us from all our subsequent abberations."

This picture of the Shepherd reclaiming and restoring the lost sheep is a beautiful allegory of how it feels to have been lost in the wilds, the "blind alleys" of life; to be gently pursued; and to be carried home—to the life we were intended to have from the beginning.

That we belong *with God* stems from the fact that we were created in God's image—though we may have lost our sense of that wholeness. God's reaching out to bring us back, into the awareness of our belonging, is rooted in the nature of God—the immeasurable, never-failing love of Creator for creature. The necessity of such a rescue is based on our own propensity to stray from the best path for our soul, to fall into destructive, self-defeating behaviors.

The choice to seek the guidance of our Shepherd marks the point at which each of us became willing to admit that we didn't have all the answers, that we were indeed needy. *And we were willing to be helped.* So we brought ourselves to ask (or allowed others to carry us, or hand us crutches, or come to our sickbed of need) so that we could gradually find the strength to accept and experience new life.

We are not new people, exactly, but the same people with new awareness. We have begun now to take responsibility for our own short-comings, our failures, our attitudes. And above all, we have acknowledged that we need help from God to enjoy any progress at all in the spiritual journey we are invited to take.

Allowing God to reach down to us, acknowl-edging that God dwells within us, will always mean learning to face more and more truth about ourselves. And to go through this painful step, we need to be held and comforted and restored simultaneously. For God will always direct us toward greater awareness of the parts of our personality, our attitudes and actions, that are most hurtful and self-defeating.

And God our Shepherd will then, with gentle patience, increase our ability to trust (as we ask for guidance) so that we are able to turn more and more of these flaws or short-comings over to the divine healing which God so longs to give us. Such a period of learning and growing is our chance for a fresh start. Author Corrie ten Boom has written, "God has plans—not problems—for our lives....The life of a Christian is an education for higher service. No athlete complains when the training is hard. He thinks of the game, or the race."

Here she offers us another metaphor for the work of God in bringing us back to the divine image: that of a competition, or race. This figure of speech was also used by the author of Hebrews in these words: "Let us lay aside every weight, and the sin which so easily ensnares us, and let us run with endurance the race that is set before us, looking unto Jesus, the author and finisher of our faith" (12:1–2).

Sometimes such an example will add another dimension to our understanding of how God guides, just as in various cultures, different expressions are used by missionaries to convey God's work to the people. In countries where there are no sheep, such as Japan, for instance— where the figure of speech in Psalm 23 would seem unapplicable—it is necessary to express the essence of the promise in other terms. This version was written by a Japanese athlete who was accustomed to running alongside a pace-setter:

The Lord is my pace-setter, I shall not rush;
He makes me stop and rest for quiet
    intervals.
He provides me with images of stillness,
    which restore my serenity;
He leads me in ways of efficiency through
    calmness of mind,
And His guidance is peace.
Even though I have a great many things to
    accomplish each day,
I will not fret, for His presence is here.
    (Quoted in John Hargreaves, *A Guide
    to Psalms*, London, SPCK, 1973. Used
    by permission.)

But in this picture of care and restoration, as
in that of the Shepherd, it is extremely important
to remember that only God can be our pace-
setter and our Guide out of the rut of habit
and defeat into which we have fallen. And
when God is our Shepherd, then any return or
realization of the divine image in us will lead
us "in the paths of righteousness," for God is a
God of truth and of reality.

John Newton has written, "In general...

the Lord guides and directs his people by [enabling] them to understand and to love the Scriptures. The word of God...is to furnish us with just principles, right apprehensions, to regulate our judgments and affections, and thereby to influence and direct our conduct."

In the Gospels, Jesus refers to Himself as the Good Shepherd, or the Beautiful Shepherd. William Temple's translation of John 10:11 reads, "I am the shepherd, the beautiful one. The shepherd, the beautiful one, lays down his life for the sheep."

In the words of nineteenth-century writer Charles Kingsley, Jesus came to earth to be the One to return or restore our souls to their connection with God:

He would understand the weakness of His
    sheep by being weak Himself;
understand the sorrows of
    His sheep, by sorrowing
Himself; understand the sins
    of His sheep, by bearing all
their sins; understand the
    temptations of His sheep, by

conquering them Himself...
    that He might show himself the Good
    Shepherd.

But all this He did, even to the point of dying
for His sheep, yet without sin.

Temple has also written, "We come closest
to God not when, with our mind, we obtain a
wide conspectus of truth, but when in our
purposes we are united with his righteous
people."

This example of true, abundant life is ours as
Christians in the wider community of our
world. As God the Father restored Jesus to life
from the dead, so may our own souls be
restored and renewed through His life for us,
His righteousness that conquered sin, and His
continual love as a shepherd for His sheep.

Sometimes as Christians we may hesitate to
fully express the basis for our faith in Christ
with everyone we meet. We may not feel we
can get into some of the deeper truths of
salvation when we are seeking to help someone
simply to reach out to God—perhaps for the
first time.

Surely God understands all of our limitations and is a patient Shepherd. Yet we are all compelled to introduce others to this divine Person—our Lord, who is revealed to us more and more through the Scriptures—and invite them to join with us in searching for more and deeper truths. Then we will all grow together in the daily challenges of life and in our experience of grace each day.

*T*HOU Lord, alone, art all thy children need
And there is none beside;
In thee the blest abide,
Fountain of life and all-abounding grace,
Our source, our center and our dwelling place!
—Madame Guyon

Ask Yourself:

Am I abiding in God, through Jesus Christ, in this moment?
"O God, in the course of this busy life, give us times of refreshment and peace; and grant that we may so use our leisure to rebuild our bodies and renew our minds, that our spirits may be opened to the goodness of your creation" (*The Book of Common Prayer*, 1977).

Truly my soul silently waits for God; from Him comes my salvation (Ps. 62:1).

CHAPTER 4

TROUBLED BUT NOT FORSAKEN

Yea, though I walk through the valley of the shadow of death, I will fear no evil; for You are with me; Your rod and Your staff, they comfort me.

THE ROAD AHEAD IS DIFFICULT. THANK GOD, I DO NOT TRAVEL ALONE.

*T*HERE is nothing the body suffers the soul may not profit by.

—George Meredith

"*L*et go and let God," is an important concept to remember in our life with our Shepherd. This involves genuine trust in the goodness God desires for us, goodness which *may* lie on the other side of our present circumstances. Once again, we are called to focus on God and not on the rocky terrain or the threatening skies above us. As the ancient thinker Seneca once said, "If we let things terrify us, life will not be worth living."

There is more to our walk with God than *presence* and *comfort*, though both are implied here, in verse 4 of the Shepherd Psalm. If we are to find the place of peace in our lives, it may require trusting God to lead us through such passages as the familiar valleys of doubt, weakness, and even despair.

A close identification with God as Guide through our life's journey also means a sense of solidarity with other struggling people.

Ann and Barry Ulanov, in *The Healing Imagination*, write that such dedication to God and God's purposes "summons us to leave our familiar country and journey into the unknown toward a whole new departure-point in everything we do, and merely on the basis of a promise. The Holy bids us identify with strangers across the world who suffer with pain much the same as ours even if it sometimes becomes more dramatic.

"This is our brother who is shot down in Vietnam, our husband who is being held hostage in Lebanon, our sister who cannot feed her starving child in famine-ridden Ethiopia."

And sometimes *we* are the ones who walk through the valley that seems overshadowed by the threat of death and loss, whether it is going through the process of a painful divorce, caring for a sick or dying parent, seeking to help children with learning disabilities, or struggling with our own depression or low self-esteem. Often these real-life problems are accompanied by some form of addiction, whether it is addiction to a substance or addiction to inappropriate, self-defeating behavior patterns.

Can we truly believe that our Shepherd walks beside us through such straits? Those of us who have already seen some of the perils along the road and called out for help in our desperation have learned that the key is always *to ask*.

The road ahead is difficult. Thank God, I do not travel alone.

A. Philip Parham writes in *Letting God*:

To be picked up and carried is difficult for many of us to accept. Thoughts like "I'm too heavy" or "I'm too embarrassed" or "I'm too dignified" or "I'm not helpless" fill our minds until we have to admit: "I'm too tired; I'm too sick; I'm powerless." To surrender and submit to the strong arms of a Savior humiliates the proud but brings joy to the weary and sick.

What keeps us from being helped is our fierce self-sufficiency. Sheep are not self-sufficient: wayward, unruly, stubborn, or stupid, perhaps, but hardly autonomous and independent. If we do identify with animals, we like to think of ourselves as being clever as a fox, strong as a horse, wise as an owl, but it's humiliating to think we are sheep in need of a shepherd.

Yet this is exactly the realization—as this most famous psalm so beautifully reminds us—that we need to come to in order to find the help that can be ours through our own valley of the shadow of death. In the Psalms there are many references to the perils of enemies and dangers from all sides which threaten our peace and immobilize us for a time. Yet we are told in Psalm 23 to fear no evil. For in the sight of God, all of these forces, "if they are weighed on the scales . . . are altogether lighter than vapor," says Psalm 62. In contrast, God is "the rock that is higher than I . . . a shelter . . . a strong tower from the enemy"; refuge can be found in "the shelter of Your wings" (Ps. 61:2–4). And the psalmist can sing:

For You have been my defense
And refuge in the day of my trouble.

To You, O my Strength, I will sing praises;
For God is my defense,
The God of My mercy (Ps. 59:16–17).

Many people have testified that in what
seemed at the time the deepest, darkest passage
of life—a squeeze through a narrow valley in
which there was little room to negotiate or
experience any freedom at all—God was there.
Martin Luther King, Jr., wrote of his all-
demanding vocation, which eventually cost
him his life, "The suffering and agonizing moments through which I have passed over the
last few years have drawn me closer to God."

Dwight L. Moody, the famous evangelist,
has written, "The valley of the shadow holds
no darkness for the child of God. There must
be light, else there could be no shadow. Jesus is
the Light. He has overcome death." Truly He
is our Light, our Shepherd, and the One who
shelters us under almighty wings of comfort
for the duration of whatever trial or ultimate
testing we undergo.

Yet as Helen Keller, a woman who overcame
so many difficulties, has said, "Character can-

not be developed in ease and quiet. Only through experience of trial and suffering can the soul be strengthened, vision cleared, ambition inspired, and success achieved."

The psalmist in Psalm 119:67 says, "Before I was afflicted I went astray, but now I keep Your word." Yet simply being afflicted, even submitting to the hardship, will not guarantee that we will "learn our lesson" and come out of our difficulty as better people. The essential act is still a surrender to God our Shepherd at every step of the way—to trust that even this detour from the pleasant path, or the safe road, is somehow allowed by our God. Philosopher Blaise Pascal wrote, "God can bring good from evil, and without God we bring evil out of good." Thus, we are sometimes simply to watch and pray, for "prayer is the gate of heaven," writes Thomas Brooks, and such supplication to and dependence upon God may be the only move we dare make.

Thankfully, others do travel with us on this path—those near and far, those with more experience than ourselves, those new to the Christian life—and some who are still seeking or simply longing for relief from their troubles. Part of our growth is learning to recognize the stages of coming back to life as we experience them—learning the feel of returning to the high ground, to the level place of balance and health in our lives—so that we can spread the word honestly and accurately and bring others along with us.

Psychologists have discovered that maintaining strong and lasting friendships is one important way to reduce stress and lengthen life. In a long-term study which examined the relationship between emotional security and physical health, clinical psychologist Oakley Ray said that "the people who had a low social support system had a death rate three times as high as the people with a good social support system" (quoted in *The Tennessean*, Jan. 8, 1992).

And the functioning of that support system depends on how the individual relates to friends, family, and colleagues, said Ray. A positive attitude—one of seeking healing for others as well as oneself—is a sure life-bringing and life-enhancing spirit.

One executive who was seeking to put his beliefs into practice in a practical way, to benefit others around him, wrote the following personal "mission statement":

I have charity: I seek out and love the one— each one—regardless of his situation.

I sacrifice: I devote my time, talents, and resources to my mission.

I inspire: I teach by example that we are all children of a loving Heavenly Father and that every Goliath can be overcome.

I am impactful: What I do makes a difference in the lives of others.

(*The Seven Habits of Highly Effective People*, Stephen R. Covey)

Why is God allowing me to go through this valley of loss and despair? we may ask. Sometimes it may feel as though God is prodding us forward into even greater danger: we feel the Shepherd's *rod.* Yet also mentioned in Psalm 23 is the *staff* of comfort.

Former shepherd Phillip Keller writes in his book *A Shepherd Looks at Psalm 23:* "The staff is essentially a symbol of the concern, the compassion that a shepherd has for his charges. No other single word can better describe its function on behalf of the flock than that it is for their comfort. Whereas the rod conveys the concept of authority, of power, of discipline, of defence against danger, the word 'staff' speaks of all that is longsuffering and kind."

And John Hooper explains, "The rod chasteneth me when I go astray, and thy staff stayeth me when I should fall—two things most necessary for me, good Lord; the one to call me from my fault and error, and the other to keep me in thy truth and verity."

Even these most trying times are a reminder that God is still present in our lives, that we do not journey alone, and that God's purposes are still being carried out even through the blackest night. It has something to do with our being witnesses to God's power—to being agents of redemption to a sinful world, in the name of Jesus.

T. R. Milford writes in *Foolishness to the Greeks:*

That is what Christians are for. A Christian is a two-edged being, rooted at the bottom in daily life ... and reaching at the other into God, whose life is eternal. The Christian is the connecting link between the two. He is like the trolley-car, which must be in contact with the conductor and also earthed, otherwise the power will not flow. As the old lady said to the policeman, "Is it dangerous to tread on this rail?" "No, Ma'am," he answered, "not unless your other foot is on that wire overhead."

Ask Yourself:

Am I willing to live as a connector between others and God, between earthly life and eternity, in order to bring others along on the journey with my Shepherd?

"Eternity is not something that begins after you are dead. It is going on all the time. We are in it now" (Charlotte Perkins Gilman).

How can I tell my own story of God's preservation of my life through the valley of the shadow of death in a way which will renew faith, help other Davids defeat Goliaths, and glorify God who is the same yesterday, today, and forever?

CHAPTER 5

A WELL-ATTENDED FEAST

You prepare a table before me in the presence of my enemies.

ALL THE PATHS OF TRUE
SEEKERS AFTER GOD
WILL LEAD TO A GREATER
ABILITY TO LOVE AND
BE LOVED.

*I*F God seems far away, who moved?
—Unknown

*S*OME fragrance always remains on the hand
that offers the rose.
—Traditional proverb

*E*arnie Larsen and Carol Hegarty tell in their book *Believing in Myself* of a man who had an eye-opening experience. While on a business trip to Chicago, he decided to go out for an early morning stroll through the downtown streets. But it became increasingly clear to him that other people were slightly stepping aside as they neared him. Some, as soon as they came close to him, would avert their eyes and avoid any contact, sometimes even stepping off the curb.

He started to become irritated, then plain angry. Who did they think they were? He felt somehow unclean, unworthy. His self-esteem, which had begun on a high note that morning, sunk to zero.

Then he decided to ask what this reaction might be saying about *him*. "Stopping at a coffee shop to lick his wounded self-confidence and warm up," they write, "he caught sight of himself in a large mirror. Then he understood! As friendly as he knew himself to be on the inside, his outside told a different story. He had forgotten to shave—a worse effect in some men than others. His hair was a mess, and his eyes were puffy and bloodshot due to the extra-long hours he had spent at a meeting the night before.

"*He* knew who he was inside, but now he got a look at how others saw his outside." *Who would you see if you saw yourself walking your way?* the authors ask.

It is sometimes easy to blame others for the kind of treatment we are getting. It is common to look at other people as enemies who simply make *our* way in the world more difficult. But a restoration to God's way gives us a chance to take another approach. By grace we can begin to look at ourselves, try to discover what is God's point of view toward all humanity, and then focus on the promise of divine concern for *all people* and their needs.

"You prepare a table before me in the presence of my enemies." Verse 5 of Psalm 23 probably refers to the Old Testament custom of presenting a thank offering to God as a sacrificial meal (see Lev. 7:11–17). But in the psalmist's depiction of the scene, the tables are turned and *God is the Host*, providing the worshiper with a bountiful spread of food in the presence of those who do not yet partake.

Yet for us, a solitary meal is not the ultimate satisfying experience. We know from Scripture that our goal is for the word to be spread, for the gifts of God's peace and healing in this life to be shared with all willing others. The bounty we have been given is to be passed around and multiplied like the five loaves and two small fishes which Jesus turned into an abundant meal to feed a multitude (see Matt. 14:17–21). God provides for such needs on a spiritual level as well. The Lord is the One who, through the ages, has "filled the hungry with good things" (Luke 1:53).

Alexander Schmemann writes in his book *For the Life of the World* that one "must eat in order to live; he must take the world into his body and transform it into himself, into flesh and blood. He is indeed that which he eats, and the whole world is presented as one all-embracing banquet table." He points out that, from Genesis and throughout the whole Bible, this image of eating remains "the central image of life . . . that you eat and drink at my table in my Kingdom."

This is the message of life which we not only enjoy but are to offer to all others we encounter as they give us any opening to share the marvelous transformation that God has begun in us; how we richly enjoy such provision for our lives; and how they too can fellowship with God and one another. It is one of Jesus' favorite expressions of the meaning of life: "come to the banquet" (see Matt. 22:4).

An exercise that can lead to growth and understanding, one that many people have discovered, is to make a list of all the persons whom you may have harmed in your life to this point. What can you do to go back and make amends, to make former enemies present friends? In this exercise you should use prudence and ask for wisdom and an opportunity, if it is God's will, to enable you to build some kind of bridge to a past failure. Sometimes it is enough to seek forgiveness before God, in the presence of a spiritual leader or counselor—and then let go of the past.

People also sometimes make a second list, this time with the names of the people who have harmed *you*. You may need to ask, *Who has hurt me in the past, and what did they do?*

The purpose of making this list is also to ultimately let go and to forgive those who have hurt you—to wipe the slate clean. But sometimes you need to acknowledge the truth: you *did* deserve better. Yet you can also see how God has worked for your good, in spite of real injury you suffered. Then with God's help, and often with the guidance of a counselor, you can let it go—and go on with your life. Such double-forgiveness gives us the chance to make up for the lost years that "the swarming locust has eaten" (Joel 1:4). In God's mercy there is time for renewal of strength and purpose, a healing of inner resentment that can immobilize us in our journey.

The Lord restores our souls, almost as though those lost years never occurred (as it sometimes seems). It is as if all that has ever happened to us and been afflicted on us can *never* obscure the love that God has shown to us. For God has invited us to the table of fellowship, spread for us even in the wilderness of our former life.

Derek Kidner writes, "The prospect is better than a feast. In the Old Testament world, to eat and drink at someone's table created a bond of mutual loyalty, and could be the culminating token of a covenant.... So to be God's guest is to be more than an acquaintance, invited for a day. It is to live with him."

St. Augustine wrote of his encounter with the living Lord, his Host: "And Thou didst beat back the weakness of my sight, shining forth upon me thy dazzling beams of light, and I trembled with love and fear. I realized that I was far away from Thee in the land of unlikeness, as if I heard Thy voice from on high: 'I am the food of [the strong]; grow and you shall feed on Me; nor shall you change Me, like the food of your flesh into yourself, but you shall be changed into My likeness'" (*The Confessions*, Book VII:10).

What keeps us from this divine encounter

that can turn enemies into friends and doubters into companions on the journey and bring us all into a greater ability to love ourselves and each other? Sometimes we ourselves—and not the other person—have been the stumbling block. It is always a good idea to take a few minutes to look in the mirror, to see whether we have been fussing too long and loud about the speck in another person's eye and have therefore entirely overlooked the huge beam of lumber (so to speak) hanging out of our own eye (see Matt. 7:4). The writers of *In God's Care* put it this way: "There's a tendency to blame people, places, and things for our problems. After all, no one as smart as us could get into so much trouble without outside help!"

They advise, "We have to quit assessing blame and take responsibility for our own actions. . . . Because all people are equal in God's eyes"—of equal worth, since all are created in the divine image—*"when we blame others for our problems we are really hurting ourselves"* (italics mine).

One thing we all need to learn is to banish

from our understanding the kind of black and white thinking which labels people *good* and *bad*, or *lost* and *saved*. It is true that some people openly deny faith in God and the fellowship that would be possible in mutual belief. We don't "sit at the same table," partly because some guests still refuse to come to the banquet (see Matt. 22:1–10).

But we are all in the process of living, and our stories are not over yet. What Jesus always taught in His parables was that *we* had better take care to be prepared for the coming of the bridegroom (see Matt. 25:1–13)—Christ Himself—the point at which the feast begins. *We* had better continue to work on our own lives and attend to *our* need for forgiveness, for improvement in right living, and for an increased ability to love as God has loved us.

Those who will come to the banquet will come... that is all we need to know for now. Perhaps it will be partly our own example of attending to ourselves rather than casting blame on others which will be the very factor that will draw them closer to the Kingdom and the Lord's table, which is ever waiting and ready to receive them.

Henry van Dyke has written of the life of fellowship and peace: "To be glad of life because it gives you the chance to love and to work and to play and to look up at the stars . . . to think seldom of your enemies, often of your friends, and every day of Christ; and to spend as much time as you can, with body and with spirit, in God's out-of-doors—these are little guideposts on the footpath to peace."

Ask Yourself:

Am I experiencing an increasing ability to forgive, and to love and cherish others, in my path of growth in Christ?

"The closed fist locks up heaven, but the open hand is an invitation to mercy" (Traditional proverb).

With which person can I begin today to open my hand, extend some act of love and kindness, and desire to learn the meaning of true forgiveness?

CHAPTER 6

ALL THAT WE TRULY NEED

You anoint my
head with oil;
my cup runs over.

AS I GROW IN
SELF-ACCEPTANCE, MY
NEED FOR PRETENSE AND
FALSITY DECREASES.

*L*OVE demands the loving deed,
 Pass it on!
Look upon your brother's need—
 Pass it on!
Live for self, you live in vain;
Live for Christ, with Him you reign—
 Pass it on!

—Author unknown

*T*HE formula for cooperating with God is this: To love God is to let God love you; to let God love you is to be completely open to what he wants to do in every part of your thinking, feeling, and attitude.

—Lloyd John Ogilvie

*"B*etter health and a longer life are the rewards for expressing fears and anger, rather than stifling these emotions," says an interesting article by Marilyn Elias in a Health column for *USA Today* (Aug. 20, 1991). This conclusion is based on the results of several long-term studies using control groups.

And, she reports, "emotional support from others can extend survival, even in the face of terminal illness," according to spokespeople for the American Psychological Association. Among reasons for longer survival of cancer patients, studies showed that these survivors were able to draw on intense support from friends and family; and all had "a quiet determination" to live.

"A 41-year study of 1,337 students by Johns Hopkins University psychologists found those who hold in tension at age 20 are twice as likely to die by 55 as peers who express anxieties or feel little tension," according to Elias's column.

It matters how we choose to live—how seriously we believe and practice the principles of love for God and for others.

And it matters whom we choose to walk alongside in our journey.

As we increasingly are able to look in the mirror at ourselves and pray for the courage and strength to allow our Shepherd to restore and renew us, we will find that we attract other people to our way of life. We become literally *attractive*.

When we are with like-minded people who admit their shortcomings and their need for God's guidance, there is a healthy atmosphere in which to air difficulties, to defuse any growing tension that we may feel is hampering us in our personal lives. And in the fellowship of other people who are seeking God also, we will find the balm of comfort through the wisdom that is available to all—and we will find as well the shared joy at triumphs and the overcoming of difficulties.

One young woman who was part of a prayer

group made up of people seeking mutual healing and sharing of God's Word had to go to her meetings on the sly. She knew that her parents would feel threatened by any knowledge of her need, any admission that *their child* had any problem or was part of anything but a perfect home. The family continued to insist that *their way* was right, that they weren't like the neighbors across the street who yelled loudly at each other or the family next door whose father and husband was gone for weeks at a time, leaving them without enough money to get by from day to day.

No, they were good, upstanding, churchgoing people who looked down on such weak folks. And meanwhile, their youngest daughter suffered silently inside, afraid to rock the boat, afraid to admit she felt stifled and false. She thought she had to protect her family's image, even though their hostility and critical spirit was literally killing her.

It was only when she reached the point of no longer feeling that she had to parent her own parents, of discovering that she was free to have needs and emotions and feelings of her own, that she sought help. And there in her prayer and healing group, she found the wonderful experience of being imperfect, but forgiven; broken, but being restored.

It makes all the difference to finally admit you *don't* have the answers, that there *are* no easy answers, but that life is a process in which we can grow *toward* the truth if we choose that path and seek it with our whole heart.

The image of anointing another with oil is a beautiful example of what one person can do to spread the joy of fellowship and healing in physical, tangible ways. It goes along closely with the image of spreading a table before our enemies and inviting others to the unending banquet of life.

"You anoint my head with oil" (v. 5) may refer to a ritual of the psalmist's day. The priest would actually pour oil over the heads of certain people to publicly signify that God was caring for them or had preserved them through some trial.

Author Leland Ryken writes in *The Literature of the Bible*, "The act of anointing with oil is readily understandable if one is familiar with the conditions of shepherding. Each night as the sheep entered the sheepfold, the shepherd examined them for injuries. The shepherd would then anoint the scratches of injured sheep with olive oil. In each sheepfold there was a large vessel filled with water. From this the shepherd would fill a large two-handled cup, from which the sheep would drink and into which a fevered sheep might sink the nose."

Ryken points out, "The image of the over-flowing cup makes most sense at this level," as applied to real practices with sheep because "when applied at a human level it evokes the picture of a sloppy host"!

Indeed, the symbol of an overflowing cup says to us in picture language that there is plenty of healing from the Source—from God the Shepherd—available to all who come. In Isaiah 61:3 we are told that the Lord is the One who will give "beauty for ashes," the "oil of joy for mourning," and the "garment of praise for the spirit of heaviness...that He may be glorified." This is a beautiful amplification of the truth that our Shepherd restores our souls by refreshing us physically, easing our fears, accepting us among others who also suffer or have suffered, and providing all that we need to be healed and continue on the journey in joy.

If God is our Host, forever inviting us and restoring us, then we are to follow His example, to seek to proclaim the message to others as a result of our own spiritual transformation.

Charles Wesley wrote in this beautiful hymn:

> Build we each the other up:
>   Pray we for our faith's increase,
> Lasting comfort, steadfast hope,
>   Solid joy and settled peace.
> More and more let love abound:
>   Never, never may we rest,
> Till we are in Jesus found,
>   Of our paradise possessed.

Clement, one of the earliest Christian leaders in the Church at Rome, wrote a letter to the Christian community at Corinth around

A.D. 96. In this letter he used the image of the Shepherd to express God's care, in one of the earliest Christian prayers known outside of Scripture:

> May every nation come to know that you alone are God, that Jesus Christ is your servant, that we are your people, the sheep of your pasture. . . . We implore you, Lord, to help and defend us. Deliver the oppressed, pity the insignificant, raise the fallen, show yourself to the needy, heal the sick, bring back those of your people who have gone astray.

Sometimes drastic help is needed to bring back those who have wandered dangerously into great peril. Former shepherd Phillip Keller writes in his classic devotional work, *A Shepherd Looks at Psalm 23*:

> In tending my sheep I carried a bottle in my pocket containing a mixture of brandy and water. Whenever a ewe or lamb was chilled from undue exposure to

wet, cold weather, I would pour a few spoonfuls down its throat. In a matter of minutes the chilled creature would be on its feet and full of renewed energy. . . . The lambs would wiggle their tails with joyous excitement as the warmth from the brandy spread through their bodies.

The important thing for me was to be there on time, to find the frozen, chilled sheep before it was too late. I had to be in the storm with them, alert to every one that was in distress. Some of the most vivid memories of my sheep ranching days are wrapped around the awful storms my flock and I went through together.

Yet in this lesson from a real-life shepherd, a spiritual truth is found. Keller writes, "Now no matter what storms I face, His very life and strength and vitality is poured into mine. It overflows so that the cup of my life runs over with His life."

This, he says, is part of his Christian life that brings "great blessing and benefit to others who see me stand up so well in the midst of trials and suffering."

Our concern for others is one reason that we persevere, through our own storms of life, waiting out the blizzards of others' coldness toward us, the misunderstandings which make us feel lost in a thicket of despair, the hunger and thirst of loneliness. Through our own endurance, we have begun to understand what others have undergone. Then we find ourselves more able to offer them our testimony:

At some point, we admitted that we could not save ourselves. And it was after we chose to turn our lives over to our Shepherd that we began to find the oil of healing and of gladness pouring over our spirits. And we were reawakened to life.

Ask Yourself:

How can I share the oil of gladness with someone else this week?

"Live your life that you may receive the blessings of the Lord. Then the peace of God our Father will be with you always" (Francis Paolo).

Am I still practicing denial of need in any area of my life, which might prevent me from receiving the precious gift of grace—the bountiful peace which God offers me in my very circumstances at this time?

CHAPTER 7

GRACE FOR THE JOURNEY

Surely goodness and mercy shall follow me all the days of my life.

THOUGH I HAVE BECOME
STRONGER, I MUST
REMEMBER NEVER TO
DENY MY NEED FOR
GOD'S GUIDANCE.

KEEP an open mind, and listen to the still small voice of God that I am sure speaks to thy inner self. To His loving care I commit thee. ... He will always surround thee with His love.

—Hannah Whitall Smith

HAPPINESS is neither without nor within us. It is in God, both without and within us.

—Blaise Pascal

"One of the hardest things for any of us to do is to end a relationship," writes the author of *A New Day*. The statement is true whether the relationship is with an employer, a friend, or someone to whom we are romantically tied. The author continues:

For various reasons, we often remain in damaging relationships long after we realize it's time to move on.

We may fear being alone. We may be unable or reluctant to face changes and the pain of letting go. Perhaps our sense of obligation to a person is based on guilt; for one reason or another, we feel we "owe" them.

Because of our improving self-worth, we're less willing to stay in unhealthy and damaging relationships these days. We

believe that we deserve better. We're
learning to honestly evaluate our ties with
others, putting aside rationalizations
and looking at the reality.

It is a good sign, at this stage of our journey,
to realize that God's goodness and mercy can
be with us even when we must take painful
action in our lives—like a surgeon who must
cut and hurt in order ultimately to promote
healing in the body.

We need to remain very close to God our
Shepherd at this stage of following in the way,
never forgetting that our new life of accepting
and living in God's guidance will always lead
us toward more loving and healthier relationships and commitments. And His guidance will
free us from obsessions with other people—
neurotic attachments that bog us down in our
spiritual life and are no gift to those people
whom we so "love" either.

Terence T. Gorski writes in *Understanding
the Twelve Steps* of people who "sacrifice
themselves because they believe that if they can
help one other human being, it will make their

lives worthwhile and give them meaning. This is not necessarily true. If you help other people and also work on developing yourself, you will be better people. If you help others by abandoning or sacrificing yourself to others, you will destroy yourself—and, in the long run, probably destroy everybody else around you."

He describes people who are so eager to help others and share the message of hope that they "lose themselves"—in the wrong sense. Without a strong enough sense of self, as someone who is whole yet still being restored, they are unable to truly help others.

Jesus in His ministry restated the Great Commandment on which the Jewish faith was built: "You shall love the LORD your God with all your heart, with all your soul, and with all your mind" (Matt. 22:37). And the corollary to it was "You shall love your neighbor as yourself" (v. 39). *In order to truly love your neighbor, you must first love God; and you must love yourself—value your own soul, your life, your sanity, your gifts—because you were created in God's image.* Then you will be more strongly equipped to listen to others, to reach out with

God's help, and to extend the gracious love which has been shown to you by your heavenly Shepherd.

To truly find the green pastures and still waters in your life may mean getting back to basics: remembering what your own goal is, in the light of your awakening to God's mercy and help, here and now. Even though we can now look in the mirror and see tremendous improvement in how we look, we can feel an extra spring in our step, and we have even begun to *bless* every person whom we encounter—there is still work to do within us.

And to allow God to give us further guidance, we need a quiet time of opening our hearts to the wisdom that is available when we ask. We need constant reassurance of God's presence in our lives as we go forward in our new life.

Thomas Merton, the contemplative monk and author of many books on spirituality, wrote in his *New Seeds of Contemplation* that there are people "dedicated to God whose lives are full of restlessness and who have no real desire to be alone.... Their lives are devoured by activities and strangled with attachments. Interior solitude is impossible for them. They fear it. They do everything they can to escape it.

"What is worse, they try to draw everyone else into activities as senseless and devouring as their own." They may plan great meetings and "make a great deal of noise and roar at one another and clap their hands and stagger home at last, patting one another on the back with the assurance they have all done great things to spread the kingdom of God," Merton writes. This is fruitless activity, not true healing for themselves or others.

Well, I had quite a contrasting experience several years ago when I was privileged to attend the Founder's Day Weekend celebration at the University of Akron, Ohio, where Alcoholics Anonymous began. I do not like crowds, and I usually feel stifled and uncomfortable sitting in a room of packed-in bleachers or myriad rows of folding chairs, unable to squeeze out and leave when I want to.

But in this instance, I never had a moment of wanting to leave. There in that crowded gymnasium I felt a palpable sense of God's presence and of fellowship with other people who had invited God into their lives. There was a flavor of honesty, of admitting that it was our shortcomings that had brought any of us there in the first place. It was refreshing, renewing to the mind and spirit.

The fellowship of other struggling people who have turned their lives over to God is where I fit in, where pretenses are not necessary and only hinder growth. In this place—at the point of admission of need, in whatever form it takes in our own lives—God can guide and help us.

Martin Luther wrote: "Sheep, you know, are most foolish and stupid animals"—see, the metaphor does put us in our place! "Nevertheless," Luther continues, the sheep "has this trait above all other animals, that it soon learns to heed its shepherd's voice and will follow no one but its shepherd, and though it cannot help and keep and heal itself, nor guard itself against the wolf, but is dependent upon others, yet it always knows enough to keep close to its shepherd and look to him for help."

How do sheep learn the ropes? How do they discover what will sustain them and preserve them through cold and illness and pain? It is always through spending time with the shepherd.

British author Hannah Hurnard beautifully writes of the soul's relationship with God in her famous allegory *Hinds' Feet on High Places*. This great woman, author of many books and missionary to Palestine, from the day of her conversion at age nineteen, considered a set-apart time of Bible reading and quiet listening to God to be the source of her spiritual life. It was her indispensable time for receiving guidance for whatever lay ahead. So she well knew the feelings of needing to trust that her fictional character, Much-Afraid, struggled with as she sought to reach the High Places of service for her Shepherd.

"It did seem strange that even after safely surmounting so many difficulties and steep places," Hurnard writes in her allegory, "including the 'impassable precipice' just below them, Much-Afraid should remain so like her name. But so it was! ...

"'The Forests of Danger and Tribulation!'" her character says with alarm. "'O Shepherd, wherever will you lead me next?'

"'To the next stage on the way to the High Places,'" the Shepherd answers.

"'I wonder if you will ever be able to get me there?...I wonder why you continue to bother with me and don't give up the job altogether. It looks as though I never shall have anything but lame feet, and that even you won't be able to make them like hinds' feet.'"

But the Shepherd consoles her and says, "Be strong, yea, be strong and fear not." He encourages her not to try to picture what the next challenge will be like, how difficult it might be. Rather, He says, "Believe me, when you get to the places which you dread you will find they are as different as possible from what you have imagined, just as was the case when you were actually ascending the precipice."

Trust Me, is the Shepherd's word of assurance to any who fear, who struggle, who are brokenhearted.

Why is it, after we have already seen what God has done in our lives, we still balk at the next step? We fear that God can't pull it off this time! This is our cue to "let go and let God" all over again.

Then our kind Shepherd will begin to pour out the particular blessings and strength which are necessary for *us* on this stage of the journey.

The *goodness and mercy* which God promises to show us now, in our particular straits, and in future times of need, will be sufficient...all the days of our lives. We never outgrow our need to *trust God* as His people and the sheep of His pasture (see Ps. 79:13).

Ask Yourself:

What is the biggest stumbling block to my total trust in God right now?

"[The son says,] But I have come to the end of my resources. His Father said, Hast thou come to the end of My resources? Is the Lord's hand shortened? Dost thou not know Him whom thou hast believed? Art thou not persuaded that He is able to keep that which thou hast committed unto Him? Know thy Lord and thy heart shall find repose in Him" (Amy Carmichael, *His Thoughts Said...His Father Said*).

How do my occasional doubts and the frequent roadblocks on my path make me more compassionate, more able to empathize with and love others?

CHAPTER 8

COMING HOME

*A*nd I will dwell
in the house of
the LORD forever.

PERSEVERANCE AND
PATIENCE ARE POSSIBLE
BECAUSE I KEEP THE GOAL
OF LOVE FOR GOD AND
OTHERS ALWAYS IN MIND.

"I thirst," Jesus said on the Cross. He spoke of His thirst not for water but for love. This is what we are here for: to quench the infinite thirst of Jesus for souls, for love, for kindness, for compassion.

—Mother Teresa of Calcutta

*D*o not forget to entertain strangers, for by so doing some have unwittingly entertained angels.

—Hebrews 13:2

*A*round A.D. 200, a man came to Tertullian, a theologian in Carthage, with a question many people ask today. He asked how it would be possible for him to be a faithful Christian and still maintain a successful business life.

Tertullian let the man explain his point of view. The questioner knew that he was required to be totally loyal to Christ in his daily walk, yet he considered whether there might be some "reasonable compromises" which could be made in his dealings with some of the pagans with whom he still traded.

At that time, Christianity did not have a firm footing in the Roman Empire: it was made fun of by the privileged Romans, and there was still some persecution of believers. Tertullian's questioner felt stretched between the expectations of his new Christian faith and the desire to succeed financially.

"What can I do?" he asked the wise theologian. "I must live."

"Must you?" Tertullian asked him provocatively.

What does it mean to "dwell in the house of the Lord"? As the question Tertullian asked hung in the silent air between him and this man, it surely was full of meaning: fellowship with God and integrity with fellow human beings always go together. It is always *alongside others* that we learn to live in patience and perseverance for the sake of God's kingdom. That is what it means to truly live.

The promise in this psalm is that our life is both a *full* and *abundant* one: and one that will sustain us *now* and *into eternity*. The relationships and commitments which begin here are of lasting significance; therefore the call to love and honor each other in Christ is one which we must take seriously and keep in mind in all our concerns.

C. S. Lewis wrote: "You have never talked to a mere mortal...it is immortals whom we joke with, work with, marry, snub, and exploit...." It is no wonder that it is taught in

Jewish tradition (and reiterated by Jesus) that to love God "with all your heart, with all your soul, and with all your mind" is the first and great commandment. And the second is like it: "You shall love your neighbor as yourself" (Matt. 22:37, 39).

It is a lifetime task to learn how it is possible to seek to put these two commandments into practice in all our dealings. But we do know from what we have learned to this point that we must keep a close watch on the "house" of our own soul, as Anglican writer Evelyn Underhill puts it, never "forgetting our creaturely status, and the very moderate position which our small house occupies in the City of God" (*The House of the Soul*, 1929).

"Christianity insists that all we need and can assimilate can be given to us at home"—within our own soul, Underhill writes. "The Light of the human world coming to us here and now, as the Bread of Life.... 'You seek,' says de Caussade, 'the secret of union with God.' There is no other secret but to make use of the material God gives us."

And what do we discover, as we choose to

accept our own situation and count our blessings, but that very "material God gives us," our positive attributes as well as our shortcomings. Here we find, within ourselves, the essence of one person whom God wishes to use. And we accept by faith that the Lord will also *enable* us to build up our own house—which is but one, but nevertheless a *part,* of the city of God's dwelling.

On what do we feed in this house of the soul? Each person "lives on God, is 'renewed day by day by the Spirit,'" Underhill writes. She makes it clear that these provisions are "*regular plain meals,* offered and deliberately taken here and now," not occasional moments of ecstatic feelings. "By solid food, not spiritual sweets," as she puts it.

How like the care of the Good Shepherd is this image of God's nurturing each soul, each one important among the many. Our Shepherd is busy providing just the green pastures and simple fare that we need to continue on the journey—all the way home.

An appreciation of God's provision for *us*—its goodness, its sustenance, its regularity—

should help to keep us from looking on others' situations with envy or pride. We didn't get to this place on our own; *we were led*. And so may others be brought into the fold of God's care through our example of thankfulness and joy in God's presence.

When the original worshipers sang together the words of Psalm 23, it was an affirmation of just these truths. "By saying or singing these words the worshippers were again expressing their trust in God," writes John Hargreaves. "Each was saying: 'I believe that, in spite of so much uncertainty and danger, I shall never be separated from the fellowship of God, nor from the fellowship of others who worship in the Temple [the house of the Lord] as long as I live.' We note that, for them, fellowship with God and with other worshippers went together. They needed to meet other worshippers in order to maintain their confidence in God."

And so do we need the company of fellow believers and humble seekers to maintain our house properly as a place of hope and encouragement for others, a small source of light which can direct them to the true Light of Christ. According to Hargreaves, our "'house of the Lord' is not a church building, it is the world." This is our field of service and witness—whether it is expressed by practicing consistently our Christian principles in our business dealings, by helping mend family hurts through the graciousness of God's love active in us, by reaching out to another who hungers and thirsts for some good news, by being a friend to another hurting person...The list is endless.

Catherine de Hueck Doherty writes:

The essence of prayer is to hear the voice of
another, of Christ, but likewise to hear
the voice of each person I meet in whom
Christ also addresses me. His voice comes
to me in every human voice, and his face
is infinitely varied. It is present in the
face of the wayfarer on the road to Emmaus;
it is present in the gardener speaking
to Mary Magdalene, it is present in my
next-door neighbour. God became

incarnate so that man might contemplate his face in every face.

Jesus tells us, "Other sheep I have which are not of this fold; them also I must bring, and they will hear My voice; and there will be one flock and one shepherd" (John 10:16).

This is the vision for which we pray and which we seek to comprehend—a vision of healing for each heart in God's peace so that our society and our world may enjoy the unity and fellowship for which we were created. We desire truly to love God and each other mightily, until we are able—with new eyes—to see the house of our own soul as part of God's eternal city, here and now. Then we will all dwell in God's house forever.

CHRIST be with me, Christ within me,
   Christ behind me, Christ before me,
Christ beside me, Christ to win me,
   Christ to comfort and restore me,
Christ beneath me, Christ above me,
   Christ in quiet, Christ in danger,
Christ in hearts of all that love me,
   Christ in mouth of friend and stranger.
                        —Traditional prayer

Bibliography

Frederick Buechner, *The Magnificent Defeat* (San Francisco: Harper & Row, 1966).

Amy Carmichael, *His Thoughts Said...His Father Said* (Fort Washington, Penn.: Christian Literature Crusade, 1941).

Ruth Connell, *The Lord Is My Shepherd* (Winston Press, 1982).

Stephen R. Covey, *The Seven Habits of Highly Effective People* (New York: Simon and Schuster, 1989).

Esther deWaal, *Seeking God* (Collegeville, Minn.: The Liturgical Press, 1984).

Ronald E. Garman, *Rejoice* (Waco, Tex.: Word Books, 1982).

In God's Care (New York: Hazelden Harper-Collins, 1991).

Terence T. Gorski, *Understanding the Twelve Steps* (New York: Prentice Hall, 1989).

John Hargreaves, *A Guide to Psalms* (London: SPCK, 1973).

Kathleen V. Hurley and Theodore E. Dobson, *What's My Type?* (HarperSanFrancisco, 1991).

Hannah Hurnard, *Hearing Heart* (Wheaton, Ill.: Tyndale House Publishers, 1978).

———, *Hinds' Feet on High Places* (Wheaton, Ill.: Tyndale House Publishers, 1975).

Phillip Keller, *A Shepherd Looks at Psalm 23* (Grand Rapids, Mich.: Zondervan Publishing House, 1970).

George A. F. Knight, *Psalms,* Vol. 1, The Daily Study Bible Series (Philadelphia: Westminster, 1982).

Earnie Larsen and Carol Hegarty, *Believing in Myself* (New York: Prentice Hall, 1991).

C. S. Lewis, *A Grief Observed* (San Francisco: Harper & Row, 1961, 1989).

Gerald G. May, *The Awakened Heart* (New York: Harper & Row, 1991).

A New Day (New York: Bantam Books, 1989).

H. King Oehmig, *Synthesis*, April 21, 1991 (Chattanooga: Synthesis Publications).

A. Philip Parham, *Letting God* (San Francisco: Harper & Row, 1987).

Leland Ryken, *The Literature of the Bible* (Grand Rapids, Mich.: Zondervan Publishing House, 1974).

Alexander Schmemann, *For the Life of the World* (Crestwood, N.Y.: St. Vladimir's Seminary Press, 1973).

Still Life: A Book of Days (Batavia, Ill.: Lion Publishing, 1989).

Ann and Barry Ulanov, *The Healing Imagination* (New York: Paulist Press, 1991).

Evelyn Underhill, *Concerning the Inner Life and The House of the Soul* (London: Methuen & Co., 1947).